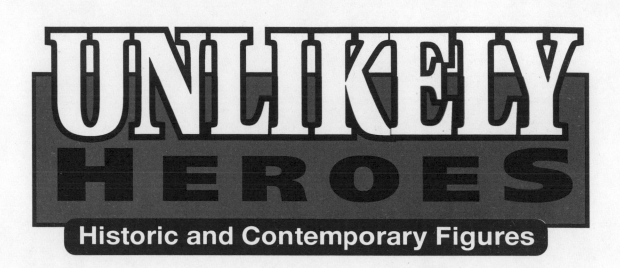

UNLIKELY HEROES
Historic and Contemporary Figures

EMMA HAHN

Contributing Author: Julie Mazur

illustrated by Carl Brand

J. WESTON
WALCH
PUBLISHER
PORTLAND, MAINE

1   2   3   4   5   6   7   8   9   10

ISBN 0-8251-2900-1

Copyright © 1997
J. Weston Walch, Publisher
P.O. Box 658 • Portland, Maine 04104-0658

Contents

Introduction . . . . *v*

Brown Weasel:
  Blackfoot Woman Warrior 1

Bessie Coleman: Daredevil Flyer 9

Annie Oakley: "Little Sure Shot" 17

Circus Heroes 25

Clara Hale: Mother to Many 33

Wilma Rudolph
  World's Fastest Woman: 39

Louis Braille: A Man of Vision 49

Crispus Attucks:
  Taking a Stand for Freedom 57

Margaret Bourke-White:
  Pictures of Courage 65

Nzinga Mbande: Freedom Fighter 73

Oseola McCarty:
  The Gift of Education 81

Introduction

There are many different kinds of heroes. They can be leaders, men or women of action, celebrities, daredevils, or just ordinary good people.

The men and women in this book are unexpected heroes: They have come from simple beginnings, and they have braved extraordinary obstacles to accomplish incredible things. Some of them have overcome poverty. Others have overcome racial prejudice. Annie Oakley grew up in an orphanage. Bessie Coleman's mother picked cotton so her children could go to school. Crispus Attucks was a freed slave who, long before the civil rights movement, took a stand for the freedom of our nation.

These stories show how all of us can be heroes in our own lives if we have the courage to stand up for whatever we believe to be good for ourselves and for others. Each of the heroes in these stories has made the world a better place for us to live in.

All of the accounts in this book are based on true stories about real people.

Brown Weasel: Blackfoot Woman Warrior

The Blackfoot were once a large and powerful Algonquian tribe located in Montana and Canada. Historians do not know for certain how these Native Americans came to be called Blackfoot. Some say that there is a legend about how the Blackfoots' ancestors walked through the aftermath of a prairie fire for so many days that their moccasins turned black. Others say that early members of the Blackfoot tribe painted their leather moccasins black. However, no evidence of black moccasins remains. And no Blackfoot can verify the accuracy of the prairie fire legend. So, the origin of the tribe's name remains a mystery.

Brown Weasel was an unusual Blackfoot girl. The eldest of four children, she was the daughter of a famous warrior. Early on, she got bored with the sewing, cooking, rawhide tanning, and child-care lessons her mother and aunts taught her. She believed her brothers had a much more exciting life. So, she asked her father to teach her how to ride horses and how to shoot a bow and arrow.

Her father knew that his daughter's request was unusual. But he loved his brave girl, and so he agreed to teach her. Soon, Brown Weasel rode as well as any boy in the camp. She became an expert with a bow and arrow. Then her father let her accompany him on buffalo hunts.

Many of the other warriors were unhappy about that. They did not think a girl belonged in their hunting parties. But one day, Brown Weasel proved her skill and courage to everyone.

That day, the Blackfoot hunting party was riding after buffalo. A band of enemy warriors attacked. The horse of Brown Weasel's father was shot. The father was left stranded on foot, surrounded by the enemy. Without a moment's hesitation, Brown Weasel turned her horse and galloped toward the enemy forces. Arrows flew all around her. Approaching her father, she grasped her pony's neck and slid over onto its side. Then she thrust out her arm. Her father grasped her arm and swung himself up onto her pony, right behind her.

It was an amazing rescue. Only the most courageous of warriors had ever attempted such a rescue. When Brown Weasel and her father returned to camp, there was a great celebration. It was a fitting tribute to a young girl's skill and courage.

Unfortunately, not long after that, Brown Weasel's father was killed in battle. Then, learning of her husband's death, Brown Weasel's mother died of a broken heart. Brown Weasel had to decide how best to care for her brothers and sisters. She chose to assume her father's warrior role. She invited an old widow to live with her family and do the household work.

Meanwhile, not everyone in the village was pleased with Brown Weasel's plans. The tribe may have recognized Brown Weasel's bravery during the buffalo hunts. But it was a whole other thing for them to accept her as a warrior. At first, the chief did not let her join the war parties. She followed them anyway. When the warriors discovered her, they ordered her to go back to camp. But she refused to go. Reluctantly, they let her come along at last.

That turned out to be a wise move. For soon, Brown Weasel proved her worth in action. A small Blackfoot war party set out to retrieve some of their horses that had been stolen by Crow tribesmen. At night, they slipped into the Crow camp and recaptured the stolen horses. Brown Weasel got 11 of them herself. But that was just the beginning.

On the way back to camp, the Blackfoot stopped one night to rest. Two Crow warriors sneaked into the campsite. Brown Weasel was on guard. First, she ran to make sure the horses were tied securely. The Crow warriors saw her but thought that since she was only a woman they had nothing to fear.

That was their big mistake. Brown Weasel shot one Crow as he tried to cut the horses free from their ropes. Then, knowing she did not have time to reload her own rifle, she grabbed the gun from the Crow she had shot. Using it, she fired at the other Crow, who by then was fleeing from the Blackfoot campsite. Brown Weasel missed him. But another Blackfoot, awakened by the commotion, shot and killed him.

Brown Weasel's people were very proud of her. On her first war party, she had not only retrieved 11 horses but also killed an enemy and captured his gun and horse. The chief and other tribal leaders decided that Brown Weasel was a special young woman. Therefore, they allowed her to undertake a vision quest—a privilege very rare for a young Blackfoot girl.

Brown Weasel consulted with the council of tribal leaders. She performed necessary preparatory rituals. Then she went into the wilderness to spend four days by herself. During that time, she received a powerful vision.

She was instructed to dedicate her life to the sun and to her people. She returned to her village and changed her dress for a warrior's clothing and a rawhide shield.

Later, at a summer gathering of many different Blackfoot tribes, Brown Weasel was asked to stand and tell about her brave deeds. The other warriors listened and then whooped and cheered. The chief gave Brown Weasel a new name to reflect her courage and abilities. From that day forward, she was known as Running Eagle.

Running Eagle fought bravely for many years. She was killed in a battle with enemy Flathead warriors. The Blackfoot brought her body home. They gave her the full funeral for a great warrior. The story of Brown Weasel has been kept alive by many generations of Blackfoot.

Activities

Recalling the Story

Answer the following questions to see how many details you can remember from the story.

1. Where did the Blackfoot live?

2. What did the prairie fire legend explain?

3. What skills did Brown Weasel learn from her father?

4. How did Brown Weasel save her father's life?

5. How many stolen horses did Brown Weasel recover from the Crows?

6. Why didn't Brown Weasel use her own rifle to shoot at the second Crow intruder?

7. What vision did Brown Weasel have during her quest?

8. What new name was Brown Weasel given?

If You Had Been in This Situation . . .

1. Can you think of another way Brown Weasel might have rescued her father?

2. What advice would you give someone who was left to take care of younger brothers and sisters?

3. Describe what you think might happen during a vision quest.

Heroic Vocabulary

Locate each of the following words in the story. Then, for each word, write a new sentence involving heroism.

- aftermath

- moccasins

- warrior

- tribute

- worth

- commotion

- quest

- rituals

- vision

- courage

Bessie Coleman: Daredevil Flier

Elizabeth "Bessie" Coleman was born in Atlanta, Texas, in 1896. She was the twelfth of 13 children. Her mother was African American. Her father was three-quarters Native American Choctaw and one-quarter African American.

The Colemans lived in an area of Texas that was known as the cotton capitol of the West. They made their living picking cotton. Eventually, the father left to return to Choctaw country in Oklahoma Indian Territory. The mother somehow continued to make ends meet by picking cotton and doing other domestic work.

When the children reached the age of eight, they generally were sent into the cotton fields to work and add to the family income. Besie Coleman, however, was so good at numbers that her mother kept her home to do the family bookkeeping.

As she grew older, Coleman did other people's laundry to earn extra money to save for her schooling. She graduated from high school and attended a teacher's college for one year. Then her money ran out.

Coleman moved to Chicago, where two of her brothers lived. She could have found a job in a factory or as a domestic worker. But she decided to become a manicurist instead. She studied at the Burnham School of Beauty Culture. She got a job at the White Sox baseball team's barbershop.

In the barbershop, she listened to men talking about their experiences fighting in World War I. She was fascinated to hear about the use of airplanes in warfare.

She decided to quit her job and go to aviation school. She had not counted on being rejected because she was black.

Fortunately, the editor of the black newspaper, *Chicago Defender,* and the president of the local bank for blacks heard of her plight. They raised the money she needed to attend flying school in France. At the school, she specialized in parachuting and stunt flying. In 1921, she became the first American to receive a pilot's license from the Fédération Aéronautique Internationale. But more importantly, she became the first licensed black pilot in the world.

Her license allowed her to fly in any part of the world. She returned to the United States to become a barnstormer. As a barnstormer, she performed in stunt-flying exhibitions and parachute jumping at fairs and carnivals all around the country. She flew a Jenny, a surplus army plane from World War I. She planned to use the money she raised to create an aviation school for black Americans.

Only 20 years had passed since the Wright brothers' first flight at Kitty Hawk, North Carolina. So stunt-flying exhibitions were big events. One of Coleman's favorite stunts was to climb 1500 to 2000 feet in the air and then put her plane into a steep nosedive. The plane gained speed as it came down. To the audience, it looked as if the pilot had lost control and the plane were going to crash nose-first into the ground. But at 100 feet, Coleman applied power and pulled back on the stick. Just in time, her plane pulled out of its dive. Then the audience cheered and applauded wildly.

Coleman often did a series of loops—large, slow-motion circles in which the plane turned upside down.

At the very top of the loop, about 1000 feet in the air, the plane seemed to hang suspended for a moment before it came down in a graceful curve.

One time when Coleman was at the top of the loop, her engine stalled. Instead of coming slowly around, her plane nose-dived toward the ground. With no engine power, the plane was out of control. Using all her strength, Coleman was able to pull the nose up until it was parallel to the ground. Just in time, she felt the wheels touch down. She had come in much too fast. But she had plenty of runway room for the plane to slow down and stop. Coleman was tremendously relieved when she stepped out of the cockpit that day. The audience, however, thought that it was all part of her act!

Coleman was always ready to fly to raise money for her aviation school. The only times she refused were when she learned the audience would be segregated. One time, she had trouble locating a plane to fly in an exhibition in Florida. Local dealers would not sell or rent an airplane to a black woman. Never one to give up easily, she asked her white mechanic to fly a plane into Florida from Dallas, Texas.

During a dress rehearsal for the Florida performance, the plane somersaulted as Coleman was pulling out of a nosedive. Coleman was thrown out of the plane. She fell to her death. Every bone in her body was broken in the fall. Her courage and her heroic struggle on behalf of other people are commemorated in the birthplace of Amelia Earhart—Atchison, Kansas. There, along with other pilots from around the world, she is honored with a plaque in the International Forest of Friendship.

Activities

Recalling the Story

Answer the following questions to see how many details you can remember from the story.

1. How many children were in the Coleman family?

2. Where did the Colemans work?

3. What special job did Bessie Coleman do at home?

4. Where did Coleman's fascination with airplanes begin?

5. Who raised the money that enabled Coleman to attend flight school?

6. What kind of plane did Coleman buy?

7. When were the only times Coleman would not perform?

8. Name the location of the plaque that honors Coleman.

If You Had Been in This Situation . . .

1. Give some reasons for or against risking your life to do stunt-flying exhibitions.

2. How do you think the excitement of flying in the early 1920's differs from that of flying today?

3. What cause or benefit would you choose if you had a lot of money to give away?

Heroic Vocabulary

Locate the following words in the story. Then, for each word, write a new sentence involving heroism.

- domestic

- manicurist

- barnstormer

- stunt flying

- parallel

- aviation

- exhibition

- mechanic

- rehearsal

- plaque

Annie Oakley: "Little Sure Shot"

The young woman who became known as the Girl of the Western Plains actually grew up in the eastern part of the United States. Annie Oakley was born August 13, 1860, in Woodland, Ohio. Her real name was Phoebe Anne Oakley Moses. Her family were Quakers. She was the fifth of eight children.

When she was nine years old, her father died in a blizzard. Her mother could not take care of such a large family by herself. So some of the children were sent to the county orphanage. Oakley was 10 when she left the orphanage to live with a farm family. The family overworked her and treated her cruelly. After two years of abuse, she ran away.

Fortunately, she found her mother, who had remarried. Once again her mother could provide a home for the children. The next four years were happy ones. Oakley had a beautiful pony. She rode the pony and performed tricks at breakneck speed throughout the countryside.

She learned to shoot her father's old rifle. She hunted birds and other game to sell at the market. Soon she became famous for her marksmanship. It was said that her birds—no matter how small—were always shot clean through the head. It was also said that she helped pay off the mortgage on her family's farm with the profits from her hunting.

At age 15, she won a match with the famous sharpshooter Frank Butler. Just a year later, they were married. They went on tour as a dual shooting act:

Butler and Oakley. They performed in vaudeville shows throughout the Midwest. Butler was 10 years older than Oakley. He taught her how to read and how to improve her marksmanship.

In the winter of 1884, the couple traveled south with a circus. In New Orleans, they saw their first rodeo: Buffalo Bill Cody's Rocky Mountain and Prairie Exhibition. Butler had by then realized that audiences were more interested in seeing Oakley by herself. He convinced Cody to hire her for his show. Butler dropped out of the act to manage her career.

Cody renamed his show Buffalo Bill's Wild West. His extravaganzas took the country by storm. Audiences were transfixed: Pony Express riders tore across the arena; Indians in war paint and feathers attacked the Deadwood Stagecoach; Buffalo Bill came to rescue.

Oakley became one of the star performers. After the grand entry parade, she ran into the arena, aimed her gun and shot at glass balls in midair. The cowgirl was quite a sight. She stood less than 5 feet tall and weighed under 100 pounds. She wore fringed skirts and vests over embroidered blouses. She wore a wide-brimmed cowboy hat with a single star pinned to the upturned brim.

After shattering the glass balls, she leaped onto the back of a pony, swung over the side, snatched her pistol off the ground, and raced around the ring, shooting at targets tossed into the air by other cowboy performers. Then she stood on the back of her galloping pony and shot the flame out of each candle in a revolving wheel.

She was popular with the other performers, too. Chief Sitting Bull joined the show for one season in 1885. Cody paid him $50 a week, plus all the bowls of oyster stew he could eat. The Sioux chief loved Oakley's daredevil spirit. He was the first to call her "Little Sure Shot."

The Wild West Show went on tour in England. British audiences were especially fond of the sharpshooting cowgirl. Even Queen Victoria loved Oakley's performance. The English, in fact, liked her better than the big showman, Cody. Cody did not like sharing the spotlight. So Oakley ended up leaving his show. She returned to the United States and joined Pawnee Bill's Frontier Exhibition.

Two years later Cody calmed down and asked Oakley to rejoin his show. She did. They went on another tour—this time to France, Spain, Italy, and Germany, as well as England.

Back in the United States, Oakley's career came to a sudden halt. While touring America, the Wild West Show's train of 26 white cars was wrecked near Danville, Virginia. Oakley was badly injured in the accident. She was never able to get on a horse again. After an extremely slow recovery, she began to perform as a western heroine in stage plays.

Later, she and Butler gave shooting demonstrations at resort hotels in New England and in the South. During World War I, they performed sharpshooting feats for soldiers in army camps across the country.

In 1922, they were in an automobile accident in Florida. As a result, Oakley was partially paralyzed and bedridden. Butler brought her back home to Ohio. She died there at age 66. Butler died three weeks after she did. They were buried near her birthplace. People everywhere mourned this little heroine who was once confined to an orphanage but who ended up having the whole world as her home.

Activities

Recalling the Story

Answer the following questions to see how many details you can remember from the story.

1. What was Annie Oakley's real name?

2. How old was Oakley when her father died?

3. How did Oakley end up in an orphanage?

4. How much did Oakley weigh?

5. What did Oakley wear on the brim of her hat?

6. Who first called Oakley "Little Sure Shot"?

7. What was Cody's payment to Chief Sitting Bull?

8. Which accident left Oakley paralyzed?

If You Had Been in This Situation . . .

1. How do you think Oakley felt about being placed in an orphanage?

2. If you were going on tour, as Butler and Oakley did, what would you change your name to?

3. How would you feel about sharing the spotlight with Oakley?

Heroic Vocabulary

Locate the following words in the story. Then, for each word, write a new sentence involving heroism.

- orphanage

- marksmanship

- sharpshooter

- vaudeville

- arena

- spotlight

- extravaganzas

- reenactmant

- feats

- bedridden

Circus Heroes

Many heroes, including the bandleader, flying trapeze artists, a clown, and a lot of ordinary people, helped save thousands of lives when the Ringling Brothers Barnum and Bailey Circus burned in Hartford, Connecticut, on July 6, 1944.

The circus had just arrived in Hartford. It was a blistering hot day—so hot that the famous clown Emmett Kelly had trouble getting his putty nose to stick. Despite the heat, nearly 7000 people crowded into the giant big-top circus tent. They couldn't wait to see the performers and the wild animals. There were 1000 animals in all, including 40 lions, 30 tigers, 30 leopards, 20 bears, 40 elephants, and a huge gorilla.

The big-top tent, at 520 feet long, was covered by the largest piece of canvas in the world. The canvas weighed over 19 tons. It had recently been sprayed with a solution of paraffin and gasoline to make it more waterproof. At the time, no one realized that this mixture made the canvas highly flammable.

Inside the tent, high rows of bleachers circled the giant ring. Folding chairs were set up on the ground right at ringside for special guests.

Little Jamie had one of those special seats. She and her two-year-old brother sat between their parents. Her father had reserved the best seats because it was her birthday. Her favorite part of the circus was watching the flying trapeze artists swing and toss each other about, high up in the big top.

Jamie was very excited. The lions had just finished their act. The Flying Wallendas were climbing up the tall poles to get in place for their high-wire performance.

Suddenly, the circus bandleader spotted a small flash of flame in the canvas over the main entrance. He quickly waved his baton and ordered the band to play "Stars and Stripes Forever." All circus people know that this song is an alarm. It is a warning that some kind of disaster is about to strike.

Immediately, the Wallendas started down from their high wire. With the clowns and crew, they tried to move the huge crowds out of the tent. People could not understand why they were being guided outside when the show had just barely begun. Then, a sudden breeze whipped the small flame into a giant sheet of fire. When the people saw the flames shoot up to the top of the tent, they panicked. They started trampling one another in their efforts to get out from under the big top.

Jamie's mom picked up her son. One of the Wallendas led them out through a side entrance. Jamie and her dad couldn't see them or anything else through the billowing black smoke. They climbed to the top of the bleachers where others were jumping to safety. Jamie was terrified. The ground seemed so far below. She froze on the top edge of the bleachers. Her father didn't know what to do.

"Throw her," someone shouted up from the ground. "I'll catch her."

Jamie looked down and saw the face of Emmett the Clown. He stretched out his arms for her.

Her father hesitated for just a second. But the flames were rapidly spreading up the wooden bleachers.

He picked up Jamie and tossed her into the arms of the clown. Her weight knocked the clown over. But he tumbled right back up on his feet. Jamie was safe.

Several people already on the ground grabbed a blanket and held it stretched tight to break the fall for Jamie's dad. He, too, landed safely.

Others were not so lucky. The fire burned through the support poles. Then the flaming canvas fell. The people inside were engulfed in flames.

Fire engines arrived quickly. But the fire spread too fast. In minutes, 168 people—one third of them children—were killed. Another 500 were injured. The smoke was so thick that firefighters could not see whether people were still inside the burning tent.

Luckily, most of the animals were safe in their cages outside the big top.

Jamie and her dad found her mother and little brother safe across the street. Certainly, it was a birthday Jamie never forgot.

Because of this tragedy, circuses rarely perform under a canvas big top today.

Activities

Recalling the Story

Answer the following questions to see how many details you can remember from the story.

1. In what month did the circus fire occur?

2. How many people were in the audience?

3. What special day was Jamie's family celebrating?

4. How much did the tent weigh?

5. Why was the canvas coated?

6. What was the alarm that the band sounded?

7. Who caught Jamie?

8. Where were most of the animals during the fire?

If You Had Been in This Situation . . .

1. What might have been done to keep people from trampling one another?

2. Think up a private signal, such as "Stars and Stripes Forever," and describe how and when you might use it.

3. What else besides a blanket could help to break a jumper's fall?

Heroic Vocabulary

Locate the following words in the story. Then, for each word, write a new sentence involving heroism.

- big top

- solution

- trapeze

- performance

- baton

- flash

- sheet

- alarm

- bleachers

- tragedy

Clara Hale: Mother to Many

Clara McBride Hale was known as Mother Hale and as the Mother Teresa of New York. She was a Harlem housewife who dedicated her life to caring for many unwanted children.

Hale was born in 1904 in Philadelphia, Pennsylvania. When she was very young, her father was murdered. And when she was 14, her mother died.

Hale's mother always had many children around. Besides four children of her own, she was always available to care for friends' and neighbors' children. But she was not just a caretaker. She taught the children the importance of self-respect. "She'd always say, I want you to hold your head up and be proud of yourself," Hale said of her mother.

Hale got married after she finished high school. She and her husband moved to New York City. He ran a floor-waxing business. But like her father, her husband died young. Hale was left by herself to raise their six-year-old son, Nathan, and five-year-old daughter, Lorraine.

Hale did not want to leave her children at home alone. So she decided to earn money by taking care of other people's children during the day. The children were only supposed to stay with her on weekdays. But many of them did not want to go home on the weekends. The parents ended up giving Hale an extra dollar or two. Then the children stayed all the time. Hale's own daughter was 11 years old before she realized that not *all* of the children were her brothers and sisters!

Hale was a proud foster mother. Every one of her 40 children went to college. And every one of them graduated. Some became singers, dancers, or preachers. Others became schoolteachers, lawyers, or doctors.

At age 65, after she had taken care of children for 40 years, Hale decided to retire from foster care. But then, a young drug-addicted woman with a baby appeared at her door. "Your daughter said I should bring the baby here," the young woman said.

In the next few days, the woman brought Hale other children as well. Word spread quickly that Hale's was a place where unwanted babies received love and shelter.

Far from retiring, Mother Hale—the name her adopted children called her—now had more babies than ever to care for. The AIDS epidemic hit hard in New York City. Hale took in HIV-infected babies as well. People asked her how she cared for these sick children. She said, "I hold them and rock them and tell them I love them. Somehow, no matter how young or how sick they are, they understand that."

In 1969, she founded Hale House. There, with the help of a small staff, she cared for drug-addicted and HIV-infected babies. By the time she died in 1992, she had taken in more than 800 of them. She rescued them from despair by restoring their health and their dignity. Her daughter, who became a doctor, carried on the rehabilitation center after her mother's death.

In 1985, President Ronald Reagan hailed Mother Hale as an American hero. And the Salvation Army awarded her two of its highest honors for humanitarian service. Dignitaries from around the world attended her memorial service in New York City's Riverside Church.

Activities

Recalling the Story

Answer the following questions to see how many details you can remember from the story.

1. Where was Hale born?

2. Why did Hale's daughter think she had so many brothers and sisters?

3. How many foster children did Hale raise?

4. What made Hale especially proud?

5. What did the woman who came to the door have in her arms?

6. What epidemic hit hard in New York?

7. Which president honored Hale?

8. Who ran Hale House after Hale died?

If You Had Been in This Situation . . .

1. Can you explain why someone who lost both parents at a young age became such an ideal parent?

2. Why do you think self-respect was what Hale taught all her children?

3. For what reasons did Hale deserve the high honors she received?

Heroic Vocabulary

Locate the following words in the story. Then, for each word, write a new sentence involving heroism.

- available

- caretaker

- unwanted

- epidemic

- shelter

- staff

- rehabilitation

- despair

- dignity

- humanitarian

Wilma Rudolph: World's Fastest Woman

It was September 7, 1960. The temperature was almost 100 degrees in Rome, Italy. It was the last day of track-and-field competition in the 1960 Summer Olympics. More than 80,000 people were crowded into the outdoor stadium. They were hoping to see history being made.

American runner Wilma Rudolph was about to compete in the 400-meter relay for her third gold medal. If the U.S. team won, Rudolph would be the first American female runner ever to win three gold medals in a single Olympics. She had already won the 100-meter dash with a time of 11 seconds. She had also won the 200-meter dash in 24 seconds.

Only 20 years old, Rudolph was one of the most popular athletes in the games. Fans from around the world cheered her on as the "fastest woman in the world."

The fans waited for the race to begin. This was the first Olympics to be shown on television. Millions of people around the world were watching. The athletes paced nervously in the heat. But Rudolph sat quietly in thought. She had a lot to think about. For her, the journey to the Olympics had been an incredible struggle that was about to come to an end.

◆　　◆　　◆

Wilma Rudolph was born on June 23, 1940, in St. Bethlehem, Tennessee. She was the twentieth of 22 children born to poor, hardworking parents. She was a tiny baby. She weighed only 4.5 pounds at birth. No one expected her to live. But with constant attention from her large family, she survived. The family moved to Clarksville, Tennessee, just after she was born. The mother usually nursed her at home because there was only one doctor in Clarksville who would treat black people. The little girl survived the mumps, measles, chicken pox, and pneumonia.

Then, when she was four, she became very ill. She caught double pneumonia and then scarlet fever. Her family feared she would not survive. In time, she began to recover. But something was wrong with her left leg. It had turned inward. She could no longer use it. Her mother took her to a hospital in Nashville. It was almost 50 miles away. But it was the nearest hospital that would treat blacks. The doctors examined the little girl. They thought that she might have caught polio while she was sick.

At that time, there was no cure for polio. Most children who caught polio became crippled or died. The doctors said that with physical therapy and massage, there was a slim chance that the girl might be able to use her leg again someday. "She *will* walk again," her mother said. "I'll see to that."

Twice a week, the mother carried her daughter onto a Greyhound bus. Together they made the 90-mile round-trip journey to the hospital in Nashville for physical therapy. They always sat in the back of the bus, where all blacks had to sit. The girl struggled through painful exercises to strengthen the wasted muscles. Her whole family supported her. They took turns massaging her paralyzed leg every day at home. After two years, the doctors decided she was ready for a metal brace to help her move around. She could finally go to school.

School was not what she had hoped it would be. Her classmates made fun of her metal brace. And she could only sit and watch while they played basketball or other games. "All I want is to be normal," she thought to herself. "To be able to run, jump, play, and do everything the other kids can do!" She continued doing her leg exercises every day. But she did not see any great improvement. She became depressed and was often lonely.

Finally one Sunday, when she was almost 10 years old, her leg felt especially strong. She was on her way to church. She waited until everyone was inside the church. Then she took off her metal brace and tried to walk. Her leg trembled. But she went forward into the church. Everyone was amazed as she walked down the aisle without her brace. When she reached her family's pew, her friends and family applauded!

She continued wearing her brace as her leg got stronger. When she was 12, the brace was sent back to the hospital for good. It was the end of her sixth-grade year and the beginning of a new life.

She jumped into sports with enthusiasm. As her muscles became stronger, she discovered that she had natural athletic ability. Basketball was her favorite sport. For years, she had watched others play basketball while she sat on the sidelines. Watching carefully, she had developed a detailed knowledge of the game.

Now, she brought that knowledge to the court. She became a high school basketball star. She led her team to victory after victory. Finally, her team reached the Tennessee state championships. To everyone's surprise, her team lost. But for her, the devastating defeat turned out to be one of the luckiest days of her life.

Ed Temple was the track coach at Tennessee State University in Nashville. He was also the referee at the high school championship game. He noticed Rudolph's speed on the court. He decided that he wanted her for his track-and-field team. With Temple's help, Rudolph won a scholarship to Tennessee State University. She was the first member of her family to go to college.

Rudolph trained hard with Temple that summer. Success followed quickly. In 1956, when she was only 16 years old, she earned a place on the U.S. Olympic team. She brought home a bronze medal as a member of the 400-meter relay team. She continued to train with Temple. Four years later, she was stronger and more confident then ever.

◆   ◆   ◆

Rudolph's journey to the 1960 Summer Olympics had indeed been difficult. Now, she collected her thoughts one last time as she waited for the 400-meter relay to begin. The runners were called to the starting line. Rudolph was the fourth runner on the team. She was to run the final lap to the finish line.

The race started. Rudolph watched as her teammates gained first place. She got ready for her turn. Her third teammate ran toward her. Rudolph reached back to accept the baton—and almost dropped it! As she struggled to regain her balance, two other runners ran past her. The U.S. team suddenly was in third place! Rudolph concentrated as she ran toward the other runners. In a final burst of speed, she caught up to the other runners and pushed ahead. She reached the finish line first by a fraction of a second. The crowd roared! Wilma Rudolph had made history. She was the first female American runner ever to win three gold medals in a single Olympics!

When she returned home to Clarksville, Rudolph was greeted by a parade and banquet held in her honor. It was the first time in the town's history that black and white people had gathered together under one roof for any event. Wilma Rudolph, who they'd once thought would never walk again, had become the fastest woman in the world.

Activities

Recalling the Story

Answer the following questions to see how many details you can remember from the story.

1. When Rudolph was a child, what happened to her left leg?

2. Where did Rudolph and her mother have to travel for physical therapy?

3. Why was school a disappointment for Rudolph?

4. When was the first time Rudolph walked without her metal brace?

5. What was Rudolph's favorite sport in high school?

6. How did Rudolph gain such in-depth knowledge of basketball before she ever played?

7. What did Rudolph win at the 1956 Olympics?

8. How many gold medals did Rudolph win at the 1960 Summer Olympics?

If You Had Been in This Situation . . .

1. Why do you think Rudolph first tried walking without a brace in front of so many people she knew?

2. In what ways have television and advertising changed sports since 1960?

3. What further successes would you seek after winning three Olympic gold medals?

Heroic Vocabulary

Locate the following words in the story. Then, for each word, write a new sentence involving heroism.

- competition

- struggle

- pneumonia

- polio

- physical therapy

- paralyzed

- trembled

- devastating

- scholarship

- teammates

Louis Braille: A Man of Vision

Louis Braille was born on January 4, 1809, in Coupvray, a small village in France. He was a happy, blue-eyed baby. As a toddler, he loved to play in his father's workshop. His father was a master saddler and harness maker. The boy watched his father as he cut leather with very sharp tools. "You can watch, but you must never touch Papa's tools," his father told him.

One day his father went out to the yard and left the three-year-old alone in the workshop. The boy picked up a sharp pointed tool called an awl. He tried to imitate his father at work. The leather was too tough for him to pierce. The awl slipped and plunged into his left eye. The child screamed in pain. But there was little his family could do. The nearest doctor was 20 miles away. This was too far to go on horseback for an emergency.

There were no antibiotics or antiseptics at this time. Instead, a local woman stopped the bleeding with herbal medicine. The bleeding stopped, but the eye became infected. Then the infection spread to the right eye. Soon, the child was completely blind in both eyes. By the time he was five years old, he had lost all of his visual memory.

In those days, life was very difficult for the blind. There was no understanding of blindness. There were no schools for the blind. Blind people could not read or write. Many people treated the blind as useless idiots. Louis Braille retreated into a world of darkness and loneliness.

When the boy was six years old, a new priest moved to Coupvray. The priest visited the Brailles often. He soon realized that the blind boy was very intelligent. The priest arranged for him to become a student at the village's new school. There were no books for the blind. Students had to learn by remembering everything they heard. Young Braille had a very good memory and was an excellent student.

At the time, there was only one school for the blind in France. That was the National Institute for Blind Youth, in Paris. The teacher in Coupvray knew what a gifted student Braille was. With the help of the teacher, the priest, and his father, Braille won a scholarship to the National Institute. At age 10, he set off for a new life in Paris.

Conditions at the National Institute were grim. The building was damp and cold. Discipline was harsh, as it was in most schools at the time. The school library had only 14 books. The books were written with a special system of raised letters. They were made by pressing letters made of copper wire into the back of a page.

Students could "read" by feeling the raised letters. Reading this way was very difficult. Often, students would forget the beginning of a sentence by the time they reached the end. Students could not write for themselves since the copper wire had to be shaped into letters before it could be pressed into the page.

Most of the instruction at the school was oral. Braille remembered everything he heard. He learned to read music by ear and to play several instruments. He became an excellent musician.

One day in 1821, a French army officer named Charles Barbier visited the school. Barbier came to show the students a system of writing called night writing. This was a system of dots and dashes punched into paper. Barbier had developed night writing so that soldiers could communicate at night without speaking or lighting a match to give themselves away. As Braille watched the demonstration, he had an idea. "I am sure something like this could be used for the blind," he thought. By the time he was 15, he had developed the system that was later named after him: Braille.

He took the best ideas from several systems to create his writing system. He used six raised dots arranged in various patterns on paper. Sightless people were able to "read" by running their fingers over the combinations of dots. And they were able to write by using a simple tool. For the first time, people with impaired vision could learn to read and write by themselves.

Braille's system was supported by the students and teachers at his school. But the headmasters did not want to adopt a new writing system. They preferred to keep using the old system of raised letters. Still, Braille continued to work at the school—as a student and later as a teacher. He developed separate codes for math and even musical notation. When Braille was 20 years old, he published a book on writing words and music, using his system.

Braille did not live to see his writing system become popular. He caught tuberculosis. By the time he was 42 years old, he was very ill. That year, a group of his friends submitted a petition to the French government. The petition asked the government to recognize Braille's code as the official reading and writing system for the blind. It also requested that Braille receive the French Legion of Honor. That is the highest government award in France. The French government did not respond to the petition. On January 6, 1852, Braille died.

Six months later, his system became the official reading and writing system at his former school in Paris. After that, the Braille system became very popular. By 1990, it was being used all over the world. It has been adapted to almost every language, including Chinese and Zulu. In France, Louis Braille was finally given his reward—100 years after his death. In 1952, his remains were moved to the Panthéon, the home of France's national heroes.

Activities

Recalling the Story

Answer the following questions to see how many details you can remember from the story.

1. Was Louis Braille born blind?

2. How did young Braille learn his lessons at the school in Coupvray?

3. Where was the National Institute for Blind Youth?

4. What were conditions like at the National Institute?

5. How were books written for the students at the National Institute?

6. What gave Braille the idea for his new writing system?

7. What is the Braille system?

8. How did the headmasters respond to Braille's new system?

If You Had Been in This Situation . . .

1. How would you explain to a blind person the meaning of *beautiful*?

2. Compare the general conditions of your school with those of the school in Paris that Braille attended.

3. Describe one of your great ideas that your friends and family won't support.

Heroic Vocabulary

Locate the following words in the story. For each word, write a new sentence involving heroism.

- awl

- antibiotics

- loneliness

- scholarship

- discipline

- demonstration

- impaired

- headmaster

- tuberculosis

- petition

Crispus Attucks: Taking a Stand for Freedom

The sun was sinking as evening approached on March 5, 1770. A thin layer of snow covered Boston Common. In the town square, British soldiers and Americans colonists gathered. They eyed each other with mistrust. Men and boys carried stones and sticks. The Americans did not want the British soldiers on their land.

The British soldiers had come to Boston two years earlier. The people of Boston had not been paying their taxes to the British government. They thought the taxes were unfair. They wanted to protest the taxes. But the Americans had no representation in the British Parliament. The only way they could protest the taxes was by refusing to pay them. The United States was still a British colony. So soldiers were sent to make the colonists pay.

The British soldiers were not polite to the Americans. Often, there were small fights between colonists and soldiers in the streets. The people of Boston demanded that the soldiers be removed. But the British government would not budge. The tension continued to increase. After two years, the atmosphere was explosive. Something had to give.

Crispus Attucks walked with a group of men toward the square. Attucks was a tall man, about 47 years old. Some say he was black. Others say he was part black and part Native American. He had been a slave in Massachusetts years ago but had run away. More recently, he had been a sailor on a whaling ship. He had been at sea for a long time. When he came back to Boston, he saw the British soldiers and knew there was trouble. Attucks remembered being a slave. He knew how important it was to be free. He decided to help his new country be free as well.

As Attucks got to the square, he saw some commotion. A British soldier had struck a young boy with his musket. The crowd around the boy was angry. They yelled and threw snowballs at the soldier. Attucks walked to the front of the crowd. "We must not let the English make us slaves!" he yelled. "We want to be free! We must protest these taxes! We must fight back!" he shouted.

More and more people joined the crowd. "Yes, yes, we must fight!" they yelled. By now the street was filled with angry colonists. Attucks led them to the barracks where most of the soldiers lived. The crowd yelled and threw snowballs at the soldiers outside.

The soldiers were given orders to load their weapons. They aimed their muskets at the crowd. The colonists did not have weapons. But they were not afraid. They walked right up to the muskets and continued to yell. Attucks faced the soldiers.

Suddenly, one soldier yelled "Fire!" Shots rang out. Attucks fell to the ground. He had been shot in the chest with two bullets. Seconds later, two white men were shot and killed. Two others were fatally wounded. The crowd went wild.

In all, five men were killed. We now call this event the Boston Massacre. Later, the soldiers who had fired their guns were convicted of manslaughter. Their hands were branded as punishment.

The colonists would never forget the bravery of Crispus Attucks. He was the first to die in the fight for a free America. In 1888, the Crispus Attucks Monument was unveiled in Boston Common to honor the five men who were killed.

Activities

Recalling the Story

Answer the following questions to see how many details you can remember from the story.

1. Why were the British soldiers sent to Boston?

2. What were the colonists protesting?

3. What was the atmosphere like in Boston at the time?

4. Why did Attucks care about his country being free from British rule?

5. What did the colonists throw at the soldiers?

6. How many men were killed that night?

7. What do we now call this event?

8. Where is the Crispus Attucks Monument located?

If You Had Been in This Situation . . .

1. How else could Attucks have protested British rule?

2. As one of the British soldiers in the barracks, how might you have prevented shots from being fired?

3. Which of your beliefs are as important to you as the belief in freedom was to Attucks?

Heroic Vocabulary

Locate the following words in the story. For each word, write a new sentence involving heroism.

- colonists

- representation

- protest

- explosive

- commotion

- musket

- barracks

- massacre

- manslaughter

- branded

Margaret Bourke-White: Pictures of Courage

World War II was almost over. The Allied forces were advancing across Germany. As U.S. troops pushed forward, American photographer Margaret Bourke-White rushed to record every image. Bourke-White was the first woman photographer ever allowed to accompany U.S. armed forces. Since the start of the war, she had recorded image after image of death and destruction. She thought she had seen it all. But on April 11, 1945, she encountered images more shocking than she had ever imagined.

She came upon Buchenwald. Buchenwald was one of the Nazis' concentration camps. During World War II, more than four million Jews were killed in these camps. The Nazis also killed gypsies and political prisoners. Buchenwald was the first major camp that Americans liberated. The Nazis had left only two hours before the Americans arrived.

Bourke-White entered the camp with U.S. troops. She was not prepared for what she saw. As she approached the gate, she saw a crowd of men in prison clothes. They stared blankly at the Americans from behind the barbed wire. The prisoners saw that they were now free. But they did not react. There was neither joy nor relief in their eyes. They had seen too much. It was as if their spirits had already died. Bourke-White took a picture of them. Her picture captured their emptiness. Later, this haunting photograph shocked the world.

Bourke-White walked through the camp. She tried to photograph everything. At first, it was difficult for her to take pictures. Hundreds and hundreds of naked bodies lay in piles on the ground. Other prisoners were barely alive. But Bourke-White knew that without her photographs, no one would believe that these horrors were real. It was her duty to record the truth. She swallowed her grief and set to work.

◆   ◆   ◆

Bourke-White had always been proud of her courage when taking pictures. Born June 14, 1906, in the Bronx, New York, she was introduced to photography by her father. Her parents had taught her to be curious, hardworking, and adventurous. "Face your fears," her mother had told her, "and then do something about them." Later, Bourke-White earned a reputation as one of the most daring and dedicated photographers of her time.

Bourke-White started her career as an industrial and architectural photographer. She had always loved machines. So she started by taking pictures in steel mills and other industrial sites. In 1929, publisher Henry Luce saw some of her photographs. He liked what he saw. He offered her a job with his new *Fortune* magazine.

Even as a girl, Bourke-White knew she wanted to be different. "I want to do the things that women never do," she wrote in her diary. True to her word, she became known for taking pictures no woman—and few men—had ever taken before.

Sometimes this meant balancing on construction beams 800 feet in the sky. Bourke-White's daring attracted attention in the press. The headline of one story in the *New York Sun* read "Dizzy Heights Have No Terror for This Girl Photographer, Who Braves Numerous Perils to Film the Beauty of Iron and Steel." Bourke-White became a celebrity.

In 1930, she proposed to *Fortune* magazine that she photograph new factories in the Soviet Union. But the Soviet Union would not allow foreigners to travel freely around the country. "Nothing attracts me like a closed door," she said. She finally persuaded Soviet officials to authorize her trip. Her photographs gave Americans their first look at developing industry in the Soviet Union.

In 1936, Luce founded a new magazine called *Life*. This magazine would be the first to tell stories through photographs rather than words. Luce hired Bourke-White as one of the magazine's first four staff photographers. She was the only woman. Except for a brief period in 1940, she stayed with *Life* until she retired in 1969.

Bourke-White continued to break boundaries, both as a photographer and a woman. She helped publicize the condition of America's poor. She also traveled to Czechoslovakia and the Soviet Union to record events there.

With the start of World War II, she became the first woman photographer ever attached to the U.S. armed forces. While she was overseas, a transport ship she was traveling on was torpedoed. The ship sank. But Bourke-White survived and went on to cover the struggle of U.S. troops in Italy. In 1943, she became the first woman to accompany a U.S. Air Force crew on a bombing raid.

◆   ◆   ◆

As she walked through Buchenwald, her years of training helped her work through the horror. She forced herself to photograph the bones and skulls in the furnaces, and the ovens full of ashes.

For the rest of the world, her pictures became proof of what had happened at Buchenwald. Her images could not be denied or forgotten. Years later, they provided concrete evidence against Nazi war criminals at the Nuremberg trials. As in all of her work, Bourke-White's courage brought images of truth to the rest of the world.

Activities

Recalling the Story

Answer the following questions to see how many details you can remember from the story.

1. What was Buchenwald?

2. Who introduced Bourke-White to photography?

3. What sort of photographs did Bourke-White take at the start of her career?

4. Who offered Bourke-White the job with *Fortune*?

5. What was it about Bourke-White that attracted attention in the press?

6. Where did Bourke-White go in 1930 to photograph new industry?

7. What gender boundaries did Bourke-White break during World War II?

8. How did people react to the photographs Bourke-White took at Buchenwald?

If You Had Been in This Situation . . .

1. Name some situations in which a news photo or story is more important than a subject's right to privacy.

2. As Bourke-White's boss, what rules of safety would you have ordered her to follow?

3. How did the fact that Bourke-White was a woman influence the job that she did?

Heroic Vocabulary

Locate the following words in the story. For each word, write a new sentence involving heroism.

- concentration camp

- liberated

- barbed wire

- political prisoners

- courageous

- reputation

- celebrity

- boundaries

- transport ship

- torpedoed

Nzinga Mbande: Freedom Fighter

The band of Mbundu royalty, refugees, and raiders ran for their lives. Entire villages of people grabbed their belongings and retreated through the African forests and up steaming river valleys. They ran to escape the Portuguese soldiers who followed close on their heels. The soldiers were intent on killing their leader. Their leader was a woman called King Nzinga. The Portuguese caught and beheaded several of the Mbundu chieftains. But the Mbundu forces kept running. They finally got away by climbing down ropes into a gorge.

It was a narrow escape. But it wasn't the last for these people of the Ndongo area of Angola. United and led by the amazing woman Nzinga Mbande, they resisted the Portuguese from 1623 to 1663. Nzinga dressed herself as a man, had male "wives," and practiced both cannibalism and Christianity. She was an unusual woman living in unusual times.

Nzinga was *ngola*, or leader, of the Mbundu people for almost 40 years. The Ndongo tribal lands lay along the Kwanza River, on the southwestern edge of Africa.

Downstream, on the coast, was the city of Luanda. There, Portuguese colonists had built a thriving city of churches, markets, and government offices.

Nzinga was born in 1583, about 100 years after the Portuguese first came to Africa. She grew up as a member of the royal family of Ndongo. Her father, the ngola, saw that young Nzinga was unusually bright and strong. He trained her in the arts of politics and war. No one knew then that Nzinga would someday become queen. But women often held powerful positions in the tribes.

During Nzinga's young adulthood, her father began defending his lands against the Portuguese. When he died, Nzinga's brother became ngola and took over the fight. He hoped to build up his image with a victory over the colonists. He wanted to attack the Portuguese guns downriver.

Thinking the attack was unwise, Nzinga tried to stop it. In return, her child was killed—probably on her brother's orders. As Nzinga predicted, her brother's campaign was a failure. He lost many troops.

In 1622, the Portuguese proposed a cease-fire. They needed more time to seal their victory. The tribal elders decided Nzinga was the person to speak to the Portuguese governor. She was sent down to Luanda with a party of assistants and royal slaves.

At the governor's offices, Nzinga and her ladies-in-waiting entered a room full of beautifully dressed men and women. Portuguese priests and soldiers looked on. Africans in their native dress also watched from the sidelines.

As the crowd parted, Nzinga drew herself up to her full height. She approached the area set up for her meeting with the governor. She noticed that there was an imposing chair for the governor, but none for her. She was expected to sit on the floor with some pillows. She clapped her hands and one of her servants went down on all fours. Nzinga sat down on her new "chair." Now she could meet with the governor eye-to-eye.

During the talks, Nzinga impressed the Portuguese with her knowledge and diplomatic skills, as well as her poise. A peace treaty was made. Her visit was a success.

Nzinga stayed on with new friends in Luanda to study the Portuguese language and culture. She questioned priests and merchants about what they hoped to do in Africa. She studied the Catholic religion. She was baptized in the cathedral with Governor Correa de Souza as her godfather. Her Christian name became Ana de Souza.

While in Luanda, Nzinga saw African slaves being forced onto ships for the dreadful journey to the New World. The ships were called "undertakers" because so many slaves died during the passage.

Nzinga knew that many African chiefs had been drawn into the Portuguese slave trade in their battle to preserve their own people and lands. The idea of slavery was not totally wrong to Africans. Under some African laws, a person became a slave for causing an accident or committing a crime. It was not necessarily shameful to be a slave. Some slaves rose to high positions within the tribe.

Before long, the Mbundu and the Portuguese were at odds again. Nzinga's brother broke the treaty with the Portuguese. He was chased from his village. His people were weakened from more fighting. Nzinga lost patience with her brother's methods. It was clear to her that she must do something.

For the first time, Nzinga allied her people with a roving, cannibalistic horde known as the Jaga. The Jaga were fierce fighters. The settled Africans feared them. Some Jaga fought for the Portuguese. But others were impressed by Nzinga's willingness to adopt their often brutal customs.

Soon after the Jaga alliance, Nzinga's brother was poisoned and died. His son and heir did not live long afterward. Nzinga took full power. She began her campaign to get back her people's land. She entered into a long series of battles with the Portuguese.

Nzinga had to be both wily and fierce to keep the Portuguese at bay. She had her followers spread false rumors of her whereabouts. They sometimes said that she was already dead. She also used clever military tactics. Her warriors stalked the Portuguese soldiers and then attacked on a rainy day when their gunpowder was wet. Nzinga made the foreigners think that they had an easy fight by sending forward a small force. Then a larger group overran the soldiers. Nzinga's fighters were often outnumbered but rarely outsmarted.

During her later years of life, she rejoined the church, resumed her Christian name, and abolished human sacrifice. She also signed another treaty with the Portuguese that gave her people some autonomy.

Shortly after Nzinga died at age 81, the Portuguese managed to subjugate her people. But her life's work remained as an example of native resistance and female strength. In 80 of the 104 years following her death, a woman ruled the combined kingdom of Ndongo and Matamba.

Activities

Recalling the Story

Answer the following questions to see how many details you can remember from the story.

1. How long had the Portuguese been in Africa when Nzinga was born?

2. Who ruled Ndongo before Nzinga?

3. How many years did Nzinga rule?

4. Name a reason that someone became a slave.

5. What did Nzinga sit on during her talks with the Portuguese?

6. Name the group that Nzinga formed an alliance with.

7. How did Nzinga's brother die?

8. Name one of Nzinga's clever military tactics.

If You Had Been in This Situation . . .

1. If you were an African in Angola, how would you view Nzinga?

2. If you were a Portuguese soldier, how would you view Nzinga?

3. What do you think each side promised in reaching a cease-fire?

Heroic Vocabulary

Locate the following words in the story. For each word, write a new sentence involving heroism.

- refugees

- gorge

- diplomatic

- poise

- campaign

- wily

- tactics

- abolished

- autonomy

- subjugate

Oseola McCarty: The Gift of Education

In 1995, the people of Hattiesburg, Mississippi, learned there was a very unusual woman living among them. Oseola McCarty, an 86-year-old washerwoman, gave $150,000 to help poor students attend college.

"I hope this money can help children for years to come and make their dreams come true," McCarty told *Ebony* magazine. McCarty had to leave school at age eight to take care of her sick aunt and to help support the family. For almost 80 years, she washed other families' clothes for a few dollars a load. Her dreams had to wait . . . and wait.

Then she took action to make others' dreams come true. And, as a result, her own life changed in ways she had never expected.

McCarty's generous gift made her the center of national attention. Suddenly, everyone wanted to know this shy and modest woman. Colleges and civic groups invited her to awards dinners. Newspapers and magazines grilled her at length. How in the world had she managed to save so much money? Why did she give the money to the University of Southern Mississippi? And what was the secret of her peaceful, almost magical aura?

"I can't do everything. But I can do something to help somebody. And what I can do I will do. I wish I could do more," McCarty told *Jet* magazine. As to the $150,000, she said, "I just want it to go to someone who will appreciate it and learn. I'm old and I'm not going to live always."

McCarty wished she had been able to go to college. Had she been given the chance, she would have become a secretary or a nurse. Those were two of the few careers open to women when she was young.

When McCarty started thinking about her will, helping young black students was uppermost in her mind. The University of Southern Mississippi is just a short distance from her house. Once upon a time, the school did not admit African Americans. But with time, that changed. And McCarty figured she could help increase black enrollment.

The school's leaders were thrilled. "This is just extraordinary," President Aubrey K. Lucas said in *Jet*. "I don't know that I have ever been as touched by a gift to the university as I am by this one." It was the largest amount ever given by a black person to a Mississippi college.

Some people wished McCarty had given the money to a mainly black college. Others said earmarking the money for black students was reverse discrimination. In a way, these critics echoed those who once nagged at her for doing white customers' laundry. They were also like those who brought her their soiled clothes and then looked down on her for being just a poor washerwoman. Through it all, McCarty kept working.

Her workdays started at dawn. She washed clothes the old-fashioned way. She boiled them in a big pot with water hauled from the fire hydrant. She scrubbed the clothes on a washboard. When they were very clean, she hung them out on long clotheslines in the sun.

In the 1960's, McCarty got an automatic washer and dryer. She gave them away after using them once. In her eyes, they just didn't get the clothes clean enough.

Later, after more people got automatic washers and did their own laundry, McCarty switched to ironing. All the work was very hard on her hands and the rest of her body. Bad arthritis finally forced her to stop.

Before making her gift to the college, her life was mostly work, church, and the people she saw in her quiet daily routine. She never married or had children. She lived alone from 1967—the year her last close relative died. Over the years she had a pig named Hog, a dog named Dog, and a cow named Hazel. She rarely watched her black-and-white TV, which only got one channel. Her Bible was well thumbed. And she had only left Hattiesburg once.

McCarty saved money easily because her life was so simple. Her uncle had left her the house she lived in. She never had a car. She didn't wear fancy clothes. She worked, and she saved. At first it was pennies and nickels. Later, it was dollars.

McCarty figured she saved at least half of what she earned. She always put the rest in the bank. It mounted up, almost without her noticing. The bank people *did* notice. They suggested she move it from a simple savings account to better-paying investments. After a while, McCarty had about a quarter of a million dollars.

"There's good money in washing clothes," she told *Ebony.* "People didn't think there was money in washing, but there was. And I wasn't saying nothing."

When McCarty started thinking about her will, she got a lawyer to help her out. He put 10 dimes on the table in front of her. Each one represented a tenth of her money. He also had pieces of paper marked "university," "church," and "relatives."

McCarty chose the number of dimes to put in front of each piece of paper. She earmarked 10 percent of her money for her church, 30 percent for some distant cousins, and 60 percent for the university. The gift to the college was put in a trust fund to be given out after her death.

When word of McCarty's gift got out, reporters and well-wishers overwhelmed her. TV trucks crowded in front of her house. Celebrities praised her. People said they felt "peaceful" and "clean" just being next to her.

At first McCarty was so shy and modest she could barely answer the questions reporters fired at her. As time went on, she got more used to the attention. She had to. Bill Clinton invited her to Washington to receive the Presidential Citizens Medal. More honors followed. She collected so many plaques and medals they were put in a special room at the university.

McCarty was happy to do something for the community. She didn't see what all the fuss was about. In 1996, Longstreet Press of Atlanta published a book of her simple wisdom. In it, she said, "Building community is not that hard. It just takes ordinary friendliness. The woman who took me to the doctor when my arthritis got bad is a checkout person at my grocery store."

People's feelings about McCarty are summed up in one story that was retold in a *New York Times* article. McCarty used to be afraid to fly. So she took the train to the first few awards dinners. Then that started to take too much time. So she overcame her fear and took the plane to events with a university secretary, Jewel Tucker.

Tucker recalled that on McCarty's first flight, the plane took a sudden, steep turn. McCarty was scared and told Tucker she was afraid the airliner was going to turn over. "Not with you on it, it's not," said Tucker.

Activities

Recalling the Story

Answer the following questions to see how many details you can remember from the story.

1. How much money did McCarty donate for scholarships?

2. Why did McCarty have to leave school at age eight?

3. What did McCarty do for a living?

4. Why did McCarty finally stop working?

5. How did McCarty manage to save so much money?

6. How was President Clinton involved in this story?

7. Why did McCarty take the train to the first few awards ceremonies?

8. Who traveled regularly with McCarty?

If You Had Been in This Situation . . .

1. Can you think of a time when, by doing something for others, you were helped in a way you didn't expect?

2. If you were one of the students helped by McCarty, how would you show your appreciation?

3. Can you think of some other bits of simple wisdom McCarty might offer?

Heroic Vocabulary

Locate the following words in the story. For each word, write a new sentence involving heroism.

- generous

- modest

- civic

- enrollment

- extraordinary

- discrimination

- investments

- earmarked

- trust fund

- community